It's In The Post.........

Copyright@Michael McMahon 2010
The author asserts the moral right to
be identified as the author of this work.

ISBN   978-1-4466-2293-3

All right reserved. No part of this publication may be reproduced, stored in a retrieval system, or transmitted, in any form or by any means, electronic, mechanical, photocopying, recording, or otherwise, without the prior written permission of the publishers.

This book is sold subject to the conditions that it shall not, by way of trade or otherwise, be lent, re-sold, hired out or otherwise circulated without the publisher's prior consent in any form of binding or cover other than that in which it is published and without a similar condition including this condition being imposed on the subsequent purchaser.

Mr Camberwell

At six years of age I had already decided that I was going to be a Postman.
The thought of whistling my way through life, as the birds sang and the sun shone somehow appealed.
It was Mr Camberwell who gave me the means.

It was May. Next week it would be June.

I had started school mid-term, not long after the Easter break on account of our late arrival from tropical West Africa, and I was cold.

I had taken to wearing my black duffle coat with the six wooden buttons and loops to tie them fast whilst the other kids were running around in summer uniforms, shorts and cut-sleeved shirts. My coat was originally scarlet red but mother had had it dyed black so that I would not feel so self conscious and looked less like a boy wearing a girl's coat.

It was my maternal grandmother who had said
"The boy probably needs glasses" after she had observed me squinting at a copy of Look&Learn just inches from my face.

"He'll need good eyesight if he wants to be a Postman" she recanted, "Otherwise he will never be able to read the addresses on the envelopes."

After that she had the unnerving habit of watching me as closely as a prowling cat eyeing up a fallen fledgling as she gathered compelling evidence of my short-sightedness. Given that every member of my family were as sharp sighted as moles and wore spectacles for one deficiency or another, it was inevitable that I would have to and so an appointment was swiftly made with Mr Camberwell, Ophthalmic Practitioner, the sight doctor.

His premises were situated just off the town square in the half basement of a black and white timbered building with low ceilings and dark recesses.

The small window display featured various glass heads wearing the latest range of must-have shades, an assortment of varifocals in a display case and an advertising board with spaced out letters like an eye chart inviting you to have your vision tested today....Say aye to an eye test.

Mother guided me in my myopic state.

"Careful going down the steps" she cajoled under the assumption that since the making of the appointment, my eyesight had rapidly deteriorated and navigation was now by other sensory perception.

We descended into the establishment with a gentle jingle triggered by the movement of the door.

"Mr Camberwell will be with you shortly" the receptionist said in an almost reverential whisper after we had announced ourselves. "Please take a seat."

Mother and I sat waiting.

I had never had an eye-test before and not knowing what to expect I considered I should get in some last minute swotting.

I practised reading what I could see. The turned sign on the door read *closed*. The illuminated heading above the display cabinet read EYESrite. The brass plaque on the closed dark room door read *Mr Cecil Camberwell* followed by some lettering which was too small to pick out from where I sat. The name badge on the heavily bosomed receptionist read Yvonne, but I had already espied this on our introduction so I could not really count it. I tried to focus first with one eye, then the other, blinking like the lights in a village hall disco. This eye-test could only result in one thing, an A* pass and a gold star. No glasses for me.

The thing about myopia is that it creeps up on you like old age, and I was never actually aware that I could not see something properly because that was how it always was with me. Blurred and undefined, distant coloured blobs. Things that I could not see clearly were just too far away so I moved closer, or blindly missed them altogether.

The door opened behind the brass plaque and Mr Camberwell stepped out behind a smiling older lady clutching a handbag.

"Yvonne will sort you out with a choice of frames" he ushered and saying goodbye he turned his attentions to me.

Mr Camberwell was old, at least I thought he was old. He wore a dark suit with a mustard yellow waistcoat, a dickie bowtie, had grey hair combed over a thinning sun-kissed pate, and a long nose camourflaged by expensive gold rimmed glasses.

"Now young man" he addressed me cordially. "Shall we have a good look at your eyes?"

He beckoned me into the dark room and sat me down in a heavily upholstered leather chair which I had to climb up into. As my eyes became accustomed to the penetrating gloom I espied unfamiliar apparatus looming about me like a props store for a film set.

" Your Mum tells me that you want to be a postman" said Mr Camberwell making small talk to put me at my ease. "You will need good eyesight for that" he added as if he had been in conference with my grandmother, "Otherwise you will not be able to read the addresses".

Mr Camberwell explained things as he went along.

"Look stright ahead" he directed shining a ray gun into first my right eye then my left. He smelt of a mixture of Brylcream and pipe smoke.

"Look up. Look down"

"Now to the left.......and to the right.   Ahah"

He seemed pleased in a non-committal sort of way.

Next came the letter test chart.

"Can you read the third line down?" he asked flicking the illuminated screen passed the page that I had tried to memorise.

"Yes" I replied as efficiently as a civil servant.

"Go on then" he pressed after a moments pause when he realised that I was practising silent reading like we did in Mrs Walden's wednesday afternoon lessons after break.

"A D M U ....W" I rattled. Easy test this.

" And the next line?"

This was harder.

"E....G...er...P.....er...B....Y"

"Ok" Mr Camberwell encouraged "Let's try with these"

He swung over the arm of the apparatus like a crane operator swinging the boom and deposited a pair of industrial welders glasses over my face.

" Is it better with this?" he said slipping a lens disc into the frames which instantly sharpened the letter on the test card. " ......or this?"

A quarter of an hour later he stated the obvious and inevitable conclusion.

"Young man, you require glasses"

And so two days later and encouraged by Mr Camberwell's *Glasses give you character* speech, I became the latest family wearer of new NHS spectacles. They were round lensed tortoise shell affairs, with curled metal arms which gripped on behind my ears causing frequent abrasions and made me look like a right bookworm.

Sophisticated they were not, for seeing things they were brilliant.

I trialled my specs all weekend at home. As I walked down our road I noticed houses had numbers on their gateposts, and letterboxes. I could read the number plate on Mr Limplett's Hillman from the living room window, watch Blue Peter from across the room, spot wood pigeons cavorting in the huge oak tree from my bedroom window and see objects which previously had fuzzy edges with a new clarity and sharpness.

But Monday was looming and school.

"Hey Four eyes"

"Hey Fish eyes"

"Hey Specky Biggles" followed by the Dambusters theme tune.

"Hey Goggle Eyes "

Mrs Walden was never my favourite teacher. Mrs Walden was never anybody's favourite teacher but all fears I had about wearing my glasses in school were quickly dispelled. She was accomplished in maximum humiliation through minimum effort. There was no avoiding my unveiling.

Mrs Walden announced to the class in her authoritative do-not-mess-with-me voice that in our politically correct, sanitised world would now have teaching authorities taking defensive strategies and parents seeking her resignation.

"Silence" she barked stabbing the walking stick that she used to beat young boys with down hard several times on the pitted wooden floor boards.

"We have a duty to perform. It is quite a .....spectacle". She drew the word out as a comedian delivers his punch line.

I only ever get called my full name when someone either wants something from me or I am in trouble.

" Michael." Mrs Walden summoned. "Bring your case and come to the front"

I slowly slalomed between the desks and emerged at the front of the class bracing myself for the ridicule. I had wanted to pick the unveiling to my classmates at my own pace and opportune moment.

Mrs Walden placed her open palm on the top of my head and with practised ease pressed her thumb firmly into my temple and turned me to face my classmates.

"Go on" she ordered without the right of reply. "Put on your spectacles."

She might as well have pushed me off a high board as there was no turning back.

Red faced with embarrassment and brutally exposed against the wall length blackboard I fumbled with the case, took my glasses out from their padded protection, placed the frames over the bridge of my nose and side by side hooked the wire arms over my ears.

"There" said Mrs Walden to the class. "Michael wears spectacles"

I stood rigid, head bowed in an attempt to avoid the glares, my eyes filling up behind the glass screens. There was a short silence and then slowly someone clapped and within moments everyone else had joined in.

I made my way back to my desk bemused by the turn of events, self-conscious and shy.

Patricia Ward, the class heart-throb thought I looked cleverer than before although she never went as far as to say intelligent. Barry Loughton said they made me look older and more serious, which is something you really want to hear at the age of six, and Andy Thomas sent me a note under the desk saying I looked like Brians out of Thunderbirds. He meant Brains but then he always used to get lower than a B-minus for spelling.

My specs became a part of me. I did not go anywhere without them and they became part of my character.

"You only need them to watch TV and to read" Mr Camberwell had said, but I could not be bothered with all the putting on and taking off so took to wearing them full time and confining the case to my man-draw by the side of the bed, alongside the catapult with the broken elastic and the glob of chewing gum which had not yet lost its flavour.

On occasions I would fall asleep in them and would wake up with a rawness above my ears and a deep red ridge on the bridge of my nose where the frames had pressed into the skin, and looking like I had just taken off a snorkel mask. Sometimes my glasses got me out of fights. You just cannot hit a man in specs and besides if I had to run away at least I could see where I was going.

In later years I used them like an actor uses a prop. I had seen Tony Curtis in the Persuaders slickly whisk them off just as he went to kiss a girl and I tried it with Ann-Marie Wynn-Stanley. Unfortunately at the moment our lips should have merged and fireworks ignited, I whisked my glasses away and she shrieked in pain as the hinge cut a half inch gash across her cheek, and our romance ceased before it had began.

Years later I discovered that I did not need my glasses whilst being intimate and although clear sight is crucial during the chase, blurred canoodling and love making by touchy feel is most exhilarating.

I look back fondly to my first appointment with Mr Camberwell. He is long dead now and Ophthalmic Practitioner to a higher authority. When I was six years old he corrected my myopia gave me a character and opened my eyes literally, to a world which upto that point was colourful but fuzzy like old cinematic tapes. Years later I progressed to wearing contact lenses and the same feelings of self consciousness cauterised by Mrs Walden in that classroom came flooding back. As I walked away from the opticians I was convinced people were looking at me and muttering "He used to wear glasses you know". I saw my lenses as a maturing of my character and at the time it was a momentus decision to go bare faced again.

Nowadays I could elect to have laser eye surgery which promises near perfect vision, post restorative zap. Perhaps for me this surgery would be a step too far. Years earlier Mr Camberwell had just shone the light but did not fire.

Now he lives on in the super light weight frames that I wear for late night reading and nocturnal trips to the loo, and which I keep by my bedside but never go out in. Each time I wake and put them on I am transported from an oppressive world of indistinct shady forms, like a forest in the night, to a clear and optimistically focused world of colour, depth and shape.

I can still hear him say " Young man, you will need good eyesight if you want to deliver Her Majesty's mail, otherwise you will not be able to read the addresses"
And I reach for my glasses.

Postie to Pack Mule

Forty six years later, January 2nd. The beginning of another year.

The alarm goes off at 5.30 am and I rouse from my slumbers. The truth is I am already half awake waiting for the alarm to activate, anxious that I am not late on my first morning back at work. I respond to the over excited tones of the stand-in radio presenter, the usual one is still on his festive break, by reaching out and pressing the snooze button, muting him like a failed contestant on a television talent show. Just eight more minutes. I inadvertently pull the duvet off my sleeping spouse and up and around my own shoulders. Just eight more minutes, just enough to top up my full quota of sleep.

"What's tha'" murmurs my dormant wife. "Oooooph not that time already" and she snatches back her fair share of the tog, turns her back on the aggravation and re-enters her dream.

5.38am and DJ Happy on the radio starts up again. No putting it off this time. I peel away my side of the duvet and sit up. Blearily I reach for my spectacles that I have left positioned next to the radio alarm and feel the first chill of the morning. I stand up, wait for my knee to crack and then meander blinking and stretching to the bathroom for the relief of my early morning pee.

Half an hour later, replete with Weetabix and Typhoo and I am wiping down my bike seat ready for the short ride to the depot.

I am attired entirely in Post office property.

Thick rubber soled, black work boots embossed with Royal Mail on the heel, friction worn trousers in dark navy, a long sleeved, sky blue work shirt embroidered with RM insignia on the brest pocket, over which I have a thermal jacket, elasticated at the waist and zipped up from navel to collar, a voluminous dayglo orange jacket with reflective strips and hundreds of handy pockets, and all topped off with a very fetching regulation crash helmet that I look and feel a right donk in. The only things not stamped Royal Mail are my underpants and contact lenses.

I retrieve my bike which has been left hiding overnight amongst the wheelie bins in the shadow of the garage and wipe it down with a wad of paper towels purloined from the dispenser in the male posties rest room, and which I keep in one of my many pocket. I would put the bike in the garage and save myself this morning ritual but for the lack of space from all the useful things that tend to breed in garages. Saddle now cleared from overnight precipitation, handlebars drier than a camel's mouth, I place my large red bags in the front tray, set the lights, front and rear to bright and set off for the depot in the penetrating gloom like the Hovis boy. At least it is not raining.

Five minutes later and ruddy cheeked, invigorated by my short exertion I arrive at the depot and park my cycle amongst the collection of others.

In the yard the parking spaces have been rapidly occupied, leaving little option for late-comers but to randomly park across the front of others, use restricted spaces and block in as yet unused post office vehicles. Arguments are sure to ensue and tempers will be lost. The language will be mainly agricultural. In theory everyone should leave the depot at around the same time, after all the mis-sorts are sorted and each walk has been thrown off and packed up. In practise certain posties will have packed up ahead of others and want to get on. An early start means an early finish. Their exit is sure to be thwarted by an errant parker, an argument waiting to happen.

"Next time you block me in, leave me a f..... tin opener so I can cut my way out" as Mad Mick Maloney succinctly put it the other morning.

I head towards the doors and my frame.

"Mornin' " groans Max one of the delivery drivers from amongst a mobile barrier of yorks. These are metal cages on wheels, around a meter square and two metres high and designed for ease of movement whilst transporting the mail. Think shark cage on wheels and you are near the mark.

The yorks carry the sacks and trays of post from the central sorting offices and arrive in one load ready for local sorting. Each day the volume of post can be estimated from the number of yorks that come trundling off the tail-gate of the lorry. Most days there are several deliveries, as the different categories of mail gets prioritised through the main depots.

"Is it busy?" I ask as I step around the maze of now

empty cages.

"Busy enough" grunts Max non-committedly.

I walk into the melee of the depot and sign my name on the roster sheet and head towards my sorting frame at the end of a line of others.

" Mornin' Tazzzer"

Tazzzer looks up from his pile of envelopes and nods his acknowledgement.

"Morning Gazza"

"Hi mate" says Gazza walking away waving a mug. "Makin' tea. Do ya wanna cup?"

"I'm ok thanks" I say. "How do Dazzer?"

"Whatcha Mickey" Dazzer replies with a mouthful of buttered toast.

Tazzzer, Gazza, Dazzer. It is like the changing rooms at Tottenham.

I reach my frame and drop the two red postbags underneath the work surface, shoving them into place and out of the way with my boot. The frame is my office, the hub of my walk. From this one point I can gauge how much post I will have to deliver, how many parcels I have to manage, and roughly how long the delivery will take. It consists of hundreds of slots, one for each household on my round, and follows a logical route through the roads and streets that I cover. My walk includes one trunk road called Mulliner Road and a number of side streets and cul-de-sacs branching off like a family tree, and the set up of the frame reflects this. I start with a few businesses and shops with flats above at the beginning of my walk, turn into Frobisher Close, round the close in a numerically reverse route, back into Mulliner Rd and so on and so on. Up and down, in and out, criss-crossing.

I know the walk like the back of my hand. I should do I have been doing it for years. I know where to throw each item into each pigeon hole almost by instinct. I could probably do it with my eyes closed but at this time in the morning I would only fall asleep again. Just eight more minutes.

An hour later and I am ready for the road. I have bundled up all my bags, dropped some in the correct york for Big Al the driver to collect and deliver to my drop-off points, and loaded up my metal steed. Most outsiders think that posties just deliver what we have in the bags on the bike, but in truth the job is more intense than this and we frequently refill at designated addresses on the way around our walks. Six to eight full bags is normal.

The job has become more pack mule than postie.

Mr Morris

I cycle the short distance to the start of my walk.

The weather is fine, the sky clear and blue now that the winter sun has risen and burnt away any lingering early morning mist.

Bright but crisp is the forecast.

Not unnaturally, Posties have a minor pre-occupation with the weather.

In the depot regular conversations are heard as up-to-the minute bulletins are announced by colleagues coming in from outside.

"Raining out there"

"Need your waterproofs today"

"Like a monsoon out there."

"Forget your bike use a canoe"

Each morning I regularly tune into the TV weather girls over my tea and Weetabix, enlivened by their perkiness at such an unearthly hour, and address my attire accordingly. Experience has taught me that it is better to have the equipment on my back or on the back of the bike rather than at the back of the locker, and that there is no such garment as "all weather". Getting caught in a winter downpour with only a Royal Mail fleece for protection is both cold and uncomfortable, dampens the spirit and tends to make the walk seem longer.

No such worries today. Once I am up and running into the walk I am more likely to be shedding layers rather than pulling them on.

I quickly cover the shops and residential flats on the first floors and move on at a steady pace, rapidly emptying with each bundle the red bag wedged on the front of the bike. But I have an uneasy feeling, a niggle.
I know that within the reams of correspondence is one letter which is moving to the front of the bag and like a bone in a carelessly filleted fish, will potentially ruin my day.
  The address? 52 Mulliner Road.
  There is nothing exceptional about the property. It is a modest, slightly shabby mid-terraced property set amid a row of similar, much smarter well cared for homes and resembles a dog-eared paperback incongruously positioned amongst pristine hardbacks.
The two storey facade has a picture window on each floor with peeling, yellowing paintwork which last saw a brush when B&Q once sold a range of lead based gloss. To the right of the ground floor fenestration is a tired, black door with a cracked pane covered with a flapping piece of cardboard, and a rust encrusted wrought iron letter-box. This is positioned vertically not horizontally, and lacks its one primary function of opening readily to facilitate the smooth operation of delivering the mail in a successful glide to the mat. It snaps in its frame, chews the post as successfully as an industrial shredder and reverts to its starting position with a bite like Arkwright's till in Ronnie Barker's Open All Hours. There are other properties with similarly incovenient mail holes on my walk, which although they do not comply with exacting EC regulations on letter box conformity within the Community (and yes

there is at least one) I have come to tolerate their quirky idiosyncratic ways and managed to keep my fingers clear. Trust me there is nothing pleasurable about catching a freezing digit in a delinquent letterbox, and besides what use is a postperson with a deficiency in his directional department?

What makes 52 Mulliner Road exceptional? The occupant, Mr Morris.

I first encountered Mr Morris some years previously before I took on the walk on a permanent basis. Before then I had just done it occasionally, filling in or covering when a colleague was off sick or on holiday.

Any postperson will tell you that although delivering mail to a given address is not exactly rocket science, when you do a walk regularily you get to know the people, the hazards and the dogs.

I approached the terrace, seized the appropriate bundle of letters from the red bag, and sourced the package from my side pannier before moving towards the first address. Mr Morris hijacked me before I could reach the gate.

"About bloody time" was his opening line.

"Got here as quick as I could" I retorted chirpily ready to let him off his insolence seeing as how it was his first offence, at least with me.

" Not bloody quick enough" he griped and snatched the pen and record card that I offered him before scribbling his signature like a sulky sporting superstar irked with the PR. Then he slam-dunked the card into my hand like a basketball shooter scoring the winning shot in overtime, grabbed the parcel from my other hand and slammed closed his front door before I could wish him "Have a nice day" as sincerely as an American.

The following day I mentioned it to Tazzzer who stated "Oh that guy's a rude bastard" and I was not about to quibble.

Most people are pleasant and welcome the postie like a well-known neighbour.

Most people are willing to exchange the odd pleasantry, talk about the weather or comment on the amount of junk mail they receive.

" Not more bills".

" Nice today, may rain later".

" What more recycling? One day you will bring something useful."

Over the years I have, hand on heart, tried to be amiable and courteous to Mr Morris as I have with all my calls.

Alas, since our first encounter the rift between us has widened.

I have no time for him and him none for me. He is obstructive, rude, crude, odious, moody and cantankerous, although he does have some bad traits as well.

If his post is too large to fit through his excuse of a letter box, I knock.

If I knock he blasts away about being disturbed, and why did I not leave it on the step.

Regulations say I cannot leave it on the step for fear of theft, as he well knows.

I once tried to explain this to him and was met with a tirade loaded with expletives, a slammed door and parting shot which sounded something like "Ducking jobsworth"

One colleague left a *Called but you were out card* which met with a terse conversation with Len our depot manager and a van driver hair-tailing it to the address to re-deliver the item before Regional Office got involved.
The driver met a similar tirade and numerous expletives berating the standard of service, what thick bastards we all are, and why the Royal Mail should be privatised.
   I could refuse to deliver his mail altogether citing an aggressive and abusive reception or a letter box which breaks every dictate of Health and Safety in the Workplace. To do so would be to admit defeat and only deflect the problem. Mr Morris would have to come to the depot and nobody at the depot would thank me for that. Yet, for every Mr Morris there are numerous polite, well meaning people ready to exchange a few words, have a civilised exchange of views who make my day. So I tolerate his excesses and pray for a parcel that I have to deliver early on a Saturday morning when he wants a lie in.

   Today the package for him is a shoe-box size and requires his written acceptance.
   I harden my resolve knowing what I am about to receive and anticipate the worst kind of reception.
   True to form his irritated scrawl is accompanied by "There, now piss off"
   "It's always a pleasure" I say as the door slams.
   Neanderthal.

Mabel.

Thursday morning, mid February.
Dry, cold and bright.
I set off on my walk with the post bag heavily laden with mail and spring/summer catalogues from Tinderland the outdoor apparel stockists. This adds considerably to the weight and volume of the bags, so much so, that I have had to balance an additional sack on the metal rack over the rear mud-guard behind the saddle and wedge it between the bulging panniers. It is tied on with parcel string, for once amazingly available from the dispensing roll located outside the Registered post window. Usually there is just an empty spindle because Dave Tingly Tingle has purloined it for guy-ropes at the cub-scout camp, or Gay D for making into macrame plant pot holders. The sack should remain in place providing I am solicitous in negotiating the sleeping policemen waiting outside ASDA. Ride over them too quickly and the post leaps into the air and deposits itself in a strewn mess on the road, like the aftermath of a tornado.
I am overweight and later than usual leaving the depot.

The third call on my walk is Mabel, a nonagenarian.
Still particular about her appearance she invariably wears her favourite pink lambswool cardigan over a cotton blouse, a knee length skirt in a colour that only Grannies wear and Norah Batty style tights without the wrinkles, which vanish into a comfortable pair of worn slippers. On her head she has a carefully coiffured mop of hair, as pure

white as an Aylesbury duck, and in her left ear a hearing appliance which causes her some amount of agitation regarding volume control. She wears opaque pink framed spectacles, which when not perched on her nose magnifying her smiling eyes, dangle around her bosom on a gold chain like a mayoral trinket.

Mabel and I have an arrangement. When I have a package or parcel for her which is too large for the letterbox, I ring her doorbell and push a *Called but you were out card* through. On it I will have written the approximate time of my return because I have to pass her door on my way back to the depot, and this allows her sufficient time to put on her make-up, descend the stairs from her first floor flat and collect her correspondence without haste. The arrangement works well as I am not standing around wanting to press on with my walk, and Mabel is not rushing to gather her mail. This way we can have a chat without time pressures.
Mabel appreciates a natter as she lives on her own and seldom goes out now.

Every week, usually on a Thursday, she receives a magazine sent by her daughter in Bristol. It is second hand chick-lit, bought read and dispatched before being hand delivered by me.

"I like to keep up with the show-biz gossip." she says with a smile. " Strictly CD, that footballer Looney and his wife, and who's bonking who."

I arrive outside her door and scribble my note.
Back 11 to 11.30. See you then. and ring the doorbell. A familiar tune resonates around Mabel's hallway and I push off. Anybody watching who knew how slow Mabel

has become would think that I was playing a sick game of knock-and-run.

Today is a special day for Mabel. She is 94, and I have arranged with Big Al the van driver, to drop the boxed bunch of flowers from her daughter via Tinterflora at my last drop bag station so that I can deliver them myself , along with my own card and token present. Big Al would not wait long enough at her door and Mabel is not able to walk up to the depot to collect a parcel herself, so he readily agreed. It is one less package for him to deliver, one less stop to make.

Mabel was born in 1914. She never knew her father although she once showed me a sepia coloured photogragh of a uniformed gentleman standing rigidly beside a fireplace.

"He was gassed in the First World War" she had said matter of factly one morning previously."I was only two. He never came home. He was called Tommy, Tommy Gunn."

I thought that perhaps she was winding me up because over the years I have come to realise that Mabel has a dry wit and welcomes a bit of banter, but no her father really was Thomas Gunn.

"Gunn was my maiden name before I married my Sid and became a Peacock. Mabel Peacock. That's me."
She came over all nostalgic and then that mischievous glint. "It could have been worse, one of my girlfriends became Doris Morris." she added deadpan. "Though not married to that old git further down. I suppose you know him?"

My morning encounter with Mr Morris had yet to take

place and as I was running late his outburst could be readily anticipated.

    Mabel is frail now but good for her age and keeps on going despite the advancing years. When I first met her she was able to bound up and down her stairs like a majestic mountain goat but now she travels with a supportive stick and at an altogether more sedate pace.
    "Old age is a bugger" she confided one morning. "You don't feel old in here" she said tapping a craggy finger at her temple, "But in here." She waved a hand across and up and down her frame, "Everything starts falling apart or heading South.". She hitched up her boobs as if to emphasize the gravity.

    I continue through my walk and eventually arrive at the final pick-up point for my last drop bag.
Big Al has left Mabel's box of flowers perched on top awaiting my collection as promised.
    I load it onto my bike and work my way through the remainder of the post until at last I turn for the home straight back to the depot via Mabel's.
    Outside her flat once again, I rest my bike against the wall and turn the key which locks the rear wheel. Over the years I have known several bikes be wheeled away whilst the postie was otherwise occupied and locking it up becomes a case of habit. Baz Barrington once had to explain why his bike was nicked from outside the bookies when the bookies were not on his walk. Unsuccessful in his excuses Baz is no longer walking the walk and proved a salutory lesson to us all. I slip the key into my trouser

pocket and remove my crash lid.

   Inside one pannier I have a small present and card for Mabel and rummage about to retrieve it before grabbing the box of flowers from her daughter and ring the bell.

   Presently there is a shuffling and I hear a distant call. "Coming"

   I lean forward and shout back through the glazing. "Don't hurry"

   A painter in a speckled boiler suit walks past and seeing another bloke standing outside a doorway with a box of flowers and wrapped present impulsively comments "Hope she's worth it"

   "She is " I smirk letting him draw his own conclusions.

   "Doesn't the postman ring three times?" he ad libs before continuing on his way with a knowing smile that means he has painted his own picture of the situation.

   Mabel is moving down the last few stairs and into her hallway. I can see her shadow through the lace curtain which covers the panes of glass in her front door. " Nearly there" she calls.

   Then in an instant Mabel's life changes.

   The thud is sickening.

   Mabel somehow trips and I am less than a meter away standing helplessly on the wrong side of her door. She thuds into the frame and groans loudly.

   " Mabel" I call "Mabel. Are you hurt? Mabel can you hear me? Mabel. Mabel"

   I put down the packages and using both hands against the side of my face peer through the glass panes. I can make out a crumpled heap lying in front of the door motionless.

   "Mabel. Can you hear me?" I call again.

Nothing.

"Mabel" I shout. "Are you hurt? "

"Mabel. " My voice has become more insistent. Must stay calm. "Mabel. Can you hear me?"

"I'm bleeding" a weak voice trembles.

At last a response.

"Mabel. Can you open the door?"

"I'm bleeding"

I try the handle on the door in the vain hope that it will turn. Locked.

"Mabel. Listen to me. Can you open the door?"

Mabel has not moved her position. but at least she seems conscious.

"Mabel can you open the door?" I say slowly and deliberately my face pressed against the glass.

"There's blood" Mabel mumbles. "Blood all over".

"I know luv, but we need to open the door. Can you pass the keys through the letterbox?"

Normally letterboxes placed on the lowest part of the door are a Posties curse. Try bending down to a whole terrace of similarily placed ones with a swinging, heaving post bag and you begin to realise why Health and Safety initiatives stipulate letterboxes should be at waist height. Now this one positioned where it was, was a blessing.

I lay down on the doorstep, my face right up against the letterbox and opened the flap. Mabel's head is directly in front. She has blood running through her white hair, down her nose and across her cheeks from a hideous gash over her left eye. She looks ashen with fear and fright.

"Mabel" I say quietly " Hand me your keys".

She must have had them in her hand throughout her fall

because without hesitation she passes them through the slot.

"Good girl" I say. " Hold on I'm coming through now"
I clamber to my feet and put the key in the lock.

"Coming in Mabel" I call as the key turns and the door opens just wide enough for me to put my head around.

The scene is like something out of CSI. There seems to be blood everywhere. A steadily expanding pool of crimson plasma oozing across the grey tiled floor under Mabel's head. Dark drops have splattered along the length of the wall like a Hockney and started to run down in vertical traces as they rush to reach the floor. Mabel's handprint is impressed where she has tried to prevent her fall and then slumped down to the ground rubbing the blood into the paintwork with a stippling finish.

"Mabel, I am going to push the door" I say gently to her. I shoulder my weight against the wooden frame and shove as gently but as firmly as I dare. Mabel moans as she is edged aside and I swing around the frame and gain entry.

"Oh Mabel" I grimace as I take in the scene crouching down beside her stricken body.

" We need to call an ambulance for you" I say matter of factly.

"I'm bleeding" Mabel mutters almost incoherently.

"I know luv. " I said taking her hand and trying to reassure her. " We need to get someone to take a look at you".

"Just Issy" Mabel whispers weakly.

"We'll let Issy know" I say realising that her daughter in Bristol is not able to respond with the immediacy required. "First I'm going to ring for an ambulance."

"Ring Issy" Mabel slurs as her eyes flicker shut and she fades in front of me.

I reach for my mobile phone and ring the emergency services. Be quick I think.

Lying in front of me Mabel has not moved since she last spoke.

I take off my coat manoeuvring the phone from one hand and ear to the other as I slip out of each sleeve and place it over her to try and keep her warm.

The blood is incessant. She looks like she has been struck with a machete. There is a flap of skin the size of a tennis ball dangling over her left eye where she caught the door frame on her way to the floor and the amount of blood is hideous. She is deathly pale. I think she is going to die.

"Ambulance please."

"No, just an ambulance." The blood has run across the tiles and reached my boot.

I reel off the location address to the matter-of-fact voice.

"Please hurry." I end the call and crouch down beside Mabel.

She has gone now. Her breathing is non descript, the colour completely drained from her skin save for the deep stains of blood starting to conjeal into dark edges.

" Mabel, hang on " I say. " The ambulance is on it's way". I reach for her hand and hold it but the skin seems clammy and cold. " Hold on Mabel"

Everything is quiet. There is no passing traffic in the street outside and no footsteps echoing along the pavement as people hurry about their day. Mabel remains slumped behind the door, my coat making her look like a protected load under a tarpaulin. Should I try and move her? Make her more comfortable?

I can hear some sirens in the distance. I hope they are for Mabel. The ambulance station is a mere five minutes away on the Main road but what if they do not use that location. Surely the coordinator will have fed in the postcode to the computers and arranged for the nearest rescue team. Relief, the sirens are getting nearer.

I step over Mabel and shuffle around the door to stand outside on the pavement. The ambulance turns the corner into Mulliner Road wailing like a banshee and draws up alongside my arm-waving.

Within seconds the crew are tending to Mabel and within minutes she is lifted into the back of the vehicle, an oxygen mask over her face and blankets upto her chin. One of the crew is holding a blood-soaked bandage over Mabel's eye. I do not think she is conscious.

The doors slam shut and the ambulance wails away.

An audience has gathered and conversations ensue about what has happened.

I hear someone ask "What's going on?" "Who is it?" "Is she dead?".

Mrs Evans, Mabel's next door neighbour, recognises me and says that she will let Issy know that her mum has gone to hospital. She surveys the bloody hallway through the open doorway and says she will clear up the mess so I retrieve my coat off the staircase where the ambulance man left it, close the front door and realise that Mabel's keys are dangling in the Yale lock. Mrs Evans returns with a bowl of soapy water and several cloths so I give her the keys. Feeling nothing more can be done, I retrieve my bike key from my trouser pocket, undo the safety lock over the rear wheel and cycle back to the depot. I muse on what should have been such a special day for Mabel has turned out to be a stinker.

   A month later and Mabel has a huge crescent shaped scar over her left eye and an eyebrow slightly higher than the one over her right eye, which makes her look constantly surprised. Issy has christened her Isiah.
She has also moved into Bainsborough House the residential home further down Mulliner Road. It turns out Mabel was having frequent falls only had neglected to tell anybody. She has her own flat within the establishment and a warden called Joanne who is on hand should she fall again or need additional assistance.
Of course Mabel does not like being in the place.
"I feel I've lost my independence" she groans "And everyone is *so* old."
This time I do not think it is banter.

Boris.

Wednesday. Approaching Christmas.
The ice on this side of Mulliner Road is thick where puddles at the end of driveways have frozen into an opaque crust and resemble a skid pad. My boots crunch over the uneven surface as I drag my bike from one gateway entrance to the next. There is no riding it on these pavements unless I want to come a cropper and scatter Her Majesty's postbag in all directions.

December mornings. Twelve days before Christmas and the bags and panniers are fit to bursting with the daily increase in cards and packages intended to reach their destinations in time for the jollities.

I like this time of year. My customers seem to take more interest in the items I have to deliver. I guess it is the expectation of receiving something special rather than an ill-timed utility bill, a flier for venetian blinds or an opportunity to purchase timeshare in Andalusia. Sometimes my customers greet me at the door with a cheery,

"Good morning. What have you brought for me today?"

Parcels are the best thing to deliver. The shape is not always an indication of the item inside as bubble wrap and durable packaging can expand even the smallest of items and make it into the size of Ayrshire. Recently I had to deliver a package with the dimensions of a shoe box to Mr Murray at number 86 and before I had rapped his knocker, the door was opened and I was greeted with

"Great, my new mobile phone. I've been lost without this"

From the size of the parcel the phone must have been from the 1980s, a grey brick with a four foot retractable aerial.

Anything too large is taken on the vans and there is an on-going negotiation between the Postie on his bike and the delivery drivers as to what is deemed too large.

"Go on you take it, you're going there anyway" is the cry from the driver.

"Can't carry that with this load" is the cry from the burdened Postie.

Sometimes Lenny our manager has to arbitrate when negotiation descends to squabbling, because non-delivery is not an option. The mail must get through.

I prop my bike up against another gatepost, stop momentarily to check the address on my next bundle of letters, remove the retaining red elastic bands and walk towards Mrs Patton's doorstep. As I approach Boris releases his usual morning greeting, a single gruff growl through the double glazed unit, resonating like a distant roll of thunder.

"Grrrruu....ff" he resounds. Dog equivalent for "Postie!"

Mrs Patton comes to the door and takes the mail from me.

She is an elegant lady of a certain age, with carefully coiffured hair, a trim figure and a pleasing smile. Invariably she wears over her clothes a floral apron slung over her neck and tied tightly around her waist.

"Morning Mickey" she says. "Cold for you today"

Many of my customers call me by my christian name and comment on the weather. They know most mornings I will have correspondence to deliver and for some I may be the only person that they will speak to all day. You would be amazed how many people live alone.

" Morning Mrs Patton" I reply. "Off out wth your dogs today?"

Mrs Patton keeps two canines and walks them daily. Boris with his gruff growl and Flo who never murmurs a word, at least not at me. The dogs are like an old married couple, tolerant of each others ways and yet comforted by each others presence. They are an unlikely pairing, although more Posh and Becks than George and Mildred.

Boris is huge, a weighty Russian Terrier with thick black, tightly curled hair and the width and height of a Shetland pony. Flo is slim and demure, an angular, black and white pointed greyhound, with the girth of a pencil. Boris has the head the size of a lion and shiny black beads for eyes concealed within his hairy growth, whilst Flo has a lengthy, black tipped snout under flirty come-to-bed eyes and long lashes. Boris barges his way passed Mrs Patton plods down the two steps and nuzzles up against me demanding some attention. He leans his weight against my leg, his head somewhere around waist height and gently pushes.

"Morning Boris" I cajole rubbing both hands on what I hope are his ears. "Come to see the Postie have we?" I realise I am speaking to him like a doting aunt would a favourite infant nephew but I find I cannot help myself.

"Who's a grand old boy then?" I continue whilst Mrs Patton fingers her post.

"You don't need to worry about the cold do you? Not with all that hair. No you don't. No you don't. Not a handsome chap like you."

Boris just leans some more lapping up the attention, and I have to counter his weight by readjusting my position lest we tumble into the hebes in the terracotta pot by the door. Meanwhile Flo, standing behind Mrs Patton, watches this daily ritual from the warmth of the hallway listening like someone who already knows the punch line.

Boris continues to lean against my leg, reluctant for the patting to end. I get the feeling that he looks forward to the post coming as much as some of my other customers, although I rarely rub their ears.

Ten days to Christmas and still no break in the icy weather. A cold front straight from Russia has moved over the UK and like an unwelcome guest seems reluctant to leave. The weather people say it is a polar continental system and that the isobars are going to get closer together overnight, bringing strong icy blasts and possibly snow tomorrow.

I ride my bike carefully aware that black ice is lying in wait for the unwary.

Some more letters for Mrs Patton, a bank statement, a christmas card and a letter from the hospital. Posties get to recognise all the different forms of letters and what they contain partly through the external advertising on the envelopes and also by their shape and size and franking marks. Some households get the same letter on the same day of the week, some monthly and you get to notice the patterns.

I park my bike by the gatepost, pick out the bundle of mail from the red bag on the front and set off down the path.

I reach the front door and all is quiet. No roll of thunder through double glazing. No grrruuufff.

Mrs Patton opens her door and stands ashen faced. Flo slinks up behind her, pokes her head around her legs just to check who it is and then skulks off again to curl up in the hallway unable to comprehend.

"Where's Boris this morning?" I blurb unaware of the distress I am about to cause.

Mrs Patton just bursts into tears and sobs uncontrollably.

" Oh I'm really sorry" I say realising her loss. "What happened?"

Through her tears Mrs Patton tells me that the night before, Boris just lay down in the kitchen and was experiencing breathlessness so she called the vet. The vet said he had a racing heart and that he needed to go to the surgery for tests.

"You know he was such a large dog" Mrs Patton sobs. "It took nearly an hour to get him on the hoist and into the van. When we got to the surgery he was ever so good. No Fuss.No bother. he just let the vet examine him.....and then he... just....died... there on the table.... while I was holding his paw." Her eyes filled with tears again.

I truly felt for Mrs Patton as she relived the moment, for anyone who knows the sense of loss when a loved pet dies will understand. She had lost a companion, a faithful friend, someone she cared for, someone she talked to, someone she went walking with, someone whom she loved.

And for Flo it is the same. Forlornly lying in the hallway

she is bemused by the sudden disappearance of Boris.

I trudge away from the door heavy hearted and drained of festive feelings. I too will miss Boris.

Eight days to Christmas and the threatened snow has fallen. Weather warnings are in place in many parts of the country cautioning hazardous conditions with more to come. Do not go out unless you have to.

I park my bike by Mrs Patton's gatepost and trudge down the path leaving a trail of footprints in the soft white blanket.

The door opens and Mrs Patton in her floral apron fronts me.

"Morning Mickey. Bet you love this snow?" she says sardonically.

"Just have to get on with it" I respond. I know she wants to talk so I ask, "How are things?"

Flo sidles up behind Mrs Patton and pokes her nose around her legs.

"Ok" she responds. "We miss his presence don't we" she says rubbing Flo's ears between her thumb and forefinger.

"She's taken to sleeping on Boris's blanket and he had a toy rag doll, a horrible mankey thing, but she won't let go of it now"

"Aarr" I say with concerned understatement. "She obviously misses him"

"We went out in the car yesterday and you know how Boris always went in the back and Flo in the front, well Flo went in the back. She's never done that before. It's as if being in the same places as he used to be comforts her"

"Aarr" I say again.

"Anyway" Mrs Patton says more upbeat. "I've decided to get another dog"

"Same make and model?" I ask.

"If I can" says Mrs Patton.

We say goodbye and I trudge back down the path leaving footprints in the opposite direction.

Six days to Christmas. The polar continental system has been barged off the UK ring by a sumo of a polar maritime bringing cold, wet windy weather from the west. The snow has melted and been replaced by puddles, some as large as Lake Como.

I am wrapped up against the wet with only my face and fingertips open to the elements. I park my bike by Mrs Patton's gatepost and head lowered, traipse up the path.

"Morning Mickey" Mrs Patton states excitedly as the door opens.

"Guess what?"

I look blank, unsure where the conversation may lead, not wanting to burst her bubble. But her excitement is real.

" I've found another Boris. Well... not an actual Boris... there is only one Boris..... but another Russian Terrier pup."

"Oh that's great. Great news" I state genuinely relieved for her.

"It was on the internet. A boy puppy, ready after Christmas" Mrs Patton enthuses as she signs for her parcel where I point on my card.

"Another Russian Terrier?" I confirm.

"Yep. The real deal. I'm going to keep the presidential theme and call him Gorby.....short for Gorbychops"

The Gentlefolk at Bainsborough House

Thursday. Pleasantly warm and sunny.

The perky weather girl on Morning am says that it will cloud over later, with possible precipitation due in the evening.

The sun is low in the sky at this time of the day, so much so that I have to ride my bike one handed and shield my eyes from the piercing rays with the other. Some early drivers think I am waving to them and toot their horns in recognition, causing me momentary wobbles and duel handed corrective action as I regain my balance and guide my metal steed away from a juddering interaction with the kerb.

Many of my colleagues have ditched their bikes and prefer to use their own cars instead, a practise once frowned upon by the powers that be and with grave consequences for any perpetrators, but now actively encouraged. The bike shed at the depot now resembles a cycle graveyard as redundant red bicycles huddle together with deflated tyres and rusting chains, unused in months, forlorn symbols of modernisation and changing delivery methods.

I steer into the grounds of Bainsborough House, freewheel down the inclined paviored driveway and gently brake to a halt against a low sandstone wall which surrounds the gardens. I lean the handle bars against the gate post, recover several bundles of mail from the side pannier and break open the wrought iron gate which leads across a patioed area to the main door.

Bainsborough House is a residential home for the more mature person who value their independence but want the comfort blanket of a support system should difficulties arise. The building comprises seventy two one and two bedroom apartments, each with bathrooms, living rooms and kitchens. Most occupants are single now, mainly widows, although there are some couples, and all residents have full use of the communal areas, games room, laundry and gardens and the ongoing services of Handyman Ted and the watchful eye of Joanne The Warden.

I stride a few paces down the path and the gate slams shut behind me with the force of a pneumatic crusher as the closer fulfills its obligation and metal grinds against metal.

"Postie's here" I say to myself knowing that several residents will have already clocked my entrance in anticipation of their correspondence and will be hare-tailing it down into the foyer or loitering by their front doors ready to greet my arrival. Already there will be the usual reception committee of Mrs Porter, Daisy Crump and Percy Baxter sitting in the faux leather armchairs at reception like the waiting room at any GP surgery. Each will be impatient for their hospital appointment letter, bank statement or the reams of door to door junk mail that we Posties have to deliver advertising slimming products and invitating them to retrain as plumbers. In a few moments they will be joined by a stampede of septagenarian citizens anxious to receive a word from the outside world and will surround me clammering for news. I know how the distributor of Red Cross parcels at Colditz must have felt.

Through the plate glass window I can see the threesome as I approach but none of them makes a move to open the front door so I reach for the red button on the wall plate and press the intercom button. Joanne The Warden must be in her office as residents are under strict instructions for security reasons not to admit anybody into the building, and that includes the Postie.

"The Postie may not be the Postie" asserts Joanne, conveniently ignoring the fact that we are delivering not collecting. Percy, like a mischievous schoolboy, sometimes flouts this regulation, but only when he is sure JTW as he calls Joanne, is otherwise occupied, and leaves me feeling like a classroom squealer should she ask "Who let you in?".

"Yes?" a shrill voice crackles through the grate.

"Postie" I call and without a further hint of investigation the door clicks and I gain access ready to run rampant around the building.

"Look here's the post" states Mrs Porter with feigned surprise as if she had not seen me through the window, and unsteadily rises to her feet with the aid of her battered walking stick.

" What did you say?" says Daisy Crump.

"*Post is here*" shouts Percy pointing a craggy finger in my direction.

Then the three of them demand in one chorus.

"Have you anything for us today?"

I untie the rubber bands from the top pile and extricate the relevant correspondence. Experience has taught me that when I am tying up my bags in the depot, that I place these three addresses for Bainsborough House at the top of the pile in anticipation of my reception.

"Is that it?" says Percy disappointed with his sales catalogue for winter apparel. "No lottery cheque?"

"You would only get sackfuls of begging letters if you won" I say.

"Better that than the rubbish you bring" he says. "Don't let him in tomorrow" he jokes turning to JTW and toddling off to read about discounted thermal underwear.

"Have you signed the register?" challenges Joanne leaning through the reception window.

"Not yet" I say and move towards her office.

"Every visitor *must* sign in and out" she commands.

Mrs Porter interrupts.

"Have you asked him yet?"

"Asked me what?" I say mid signature.

"About Easter?" says Mrs Porter.

Joanne swaps her facial scowl for charm.

"Are you delivering here next week?" she says and like the Prime Minister at question time, I answer in the affirmative, wary of the challenging supplementary.

"Good. We are having an Easter bonnet competition and you have been elected as judge".

"Well....I.....I ..." and I cannot think of a reason why I should not.

"Oh will you do it?" chirps Mrs Porter momentarily squeezing my arm "Please, it would mean so much to us."

There is a healthy community spirit at Bainsborough House, where the residents respect each others privacy as well as encouraging comraderie. Nobody should live alone without the comfort and friendship of others and the Easter Bonnet competition, curry nights, old fashioned sing-songs, days out to National Trust gardens and the like give the residents an excuse to get together and have company when they want it.
How could I resist such a heartfelt plea from Mrs Porter, and after all, I wear a striking cycle helmet myself, so I know all about headgear.

Friday morning. Dull but not raining.
I carry my weatherproof coat just in case as the ever smiling weathergirl predicts showers.
I freewheel to my usual stopping point and rest the bike against the sandstone gate post, clunk through the gate and press the buzzer.
"Who is it?" crackles a voice I do not instantly recognise.
"Postie" I reply.
"Prepare to identify yourself. I am coming to the door" states the voice. No buzz of the door release mechanism.
I stand under the portico being watched by Mrs Porter, Daisy Crump and a stoney faced Percy Baxter.
A stern looking woman in a mauve cardigan, grey skirt and sensible shoes comes to the doorway and opens it just wide enough to speak through. The security chain and the door jamb partly covers her face as she demands as po-faced as a passport controller.
"Do you have your identification?"

I have been a postie for many years now and never before have I been asked for ID. The fact that I am dressed from head to toe in Royal Mail apparel usually does the job. I fiddle about inside my breast pocket and retrieve a badge taken at least ten years earlier when my hair was dark, considerably thicker and at a length that occasional cavorted with my eyebrows. I flash it at the face behind the door chain but she wants a closer look.

"Let me see it then " she reprimands.

I hand it to her between the gap in the door.

She studies the photograph carefully then my face, then the photogragh once more.

I know what is coming.

"Doesn't look much like you does it?" she declares.

"I'm a bit older now " I counter feeling that my deliveries to Bainsborough House lies in the balance.

"You need to get it updated" the Face advises "But I'll let you in this time."

The door closes momentarily as the chain comes off and then peels wide open allowing me access to the foyer.

"Wipe you feet" commands the Face.

Delivering mail has never been so difficult or fraught with protocol.

There is no movement towards me from my usual reception committee. They sit rigidly in the lounge chairs against the wall watching proceedings and not daring to utter a word.

"You need to sign the register" says the Face. "....... and see me when you leave. How long will you be?"

"About fifteen minutes" I respond.

"You better get along then" says the Face dismissing

me like an errand boy.

I unbind Mrs Porter's, Daisy Crump's and Percy Baxter's mail and hand it to them. None of them says a word apart from Percy who courageously puts his hand upto his face and mouths, "It's been like this all morning. We nearly didn't get our milk today. She scares me" and then looks away pretending that it was not him who spoke out of turn.

I complete my duties through the corridors and reflect that it is amazing how a simple change in routine can upset the atmosphere and rhythms for the residents, but at least the Face will have gone by tomorrow and JTW will be back with her own brand of welcome. Better the devil you know.

Thursday before Easter. The weather girl on Morning am is promising "*fingers crossed*" a fine Easter weekend and bank holiday Monday.

For me the day of judgement has arrived.

I leave my bike resting against the sandstone gatepost at Bainsborough House and stroll down the pathway to the intercom. Before I can press the red button the door is opened and I am greeted like a returning hero.

"Morning Mickey" smiles Joanne under a huge wide brimmed straw hat decorated with easter eggs made out of coloured foil and a brood of stuck on fuzzy felt, yellow chicks which look like they have been binge drinking tequila.

"We've got hot cross buns and coffee in the lounge and the ladies are all waiting for you."

The easter bonnet competition awaits my judging and

declarations.

    I tell JTW that I should deliver the post first and walk on through the carpeted corridors filing mail into the relevant letterboxes. The building seems funerally quiet away from the communal lounge where there is a general hubbub and noisy expectation. None of my usual letter drops are waiting at their doors to receive their mail, they are all too busy discussing millinery matters, until I arrive outside Mrs Elsie Jessops.

    "Have you anything for me today Mickey?" she asks her door fully open.

    "Just these" I reply handing her several items. "Not going to the easter bonnet competition?"

    "I am but I wanted to give you this"

    Now I may be imagining things but since I agreed to judge the easter bonnet competition about a week ago I have had more than my fair share of confectionary and patisserie related offers. The residents at Bainsborough House are more than generous at Christmas time with christmas boxes and envelopes containing notes and coins for an extra drink. Throughout the rest of the year I may receive the occasional Snickers bar or piece of chocolate cake but at this rate of offering I could well be a candidate for weight watchers.

    Mrs Jessop hands me a walnut whip.

    "Judging can be such hard work " she winks unashamedly. "I'll just get my hat"

    Nobbled by a nonegarian? Well certainly. Will it work? Well I am partial to the odd nut covered example of the confectioners art.

    We walk down the corridor together and into the

communal lounge.

"Here she comes with her toy-boy" is the greeting.

"He looks a bit out of breath" says Alice Springer."What you been doing to him Elsie?"

"Has he had a good look under your bonnet Elsie?" ribs Mrs Davies.

Elsie takes it in good sport, after all she knows she has given me a walnut whip.

I look around the room and there is a fine turn out. Everyone attending has gone to such trouble with their bonnet. There are hats of all shapes, designs and abilities. Some of the residents have gone to enormous lengths, sewing, stitching, and sticking, while others have tried hard but clearly lack the dexterity, skills and art and are no immediate competition for Stephen Jones or Philip Treacy.

JTW advises me that I need to choose three contestants and grade them third, second and the winner.

I take my time wandering around the room with my cup of tea and hot cross bun, surveying the hats on the seated ladies from the front, rear and above. I am not really sure what I should be looking for but hope that there will be a stand out entrant whom everyone else agrees should win. I commend various entries, like a headmaster at prize giving, ask how they came up with their unusual idea, or how they managed to get the stuffed rabbit to stay in position. And then I spot it. Perched on a dining chair half hidden by a pillar is the winner. I do not declare there and then but stroll about a little longer, putting on a show of making careful deliberation for a few more minutes.

JTW calls the gathering to order with a gentle tickling of teaspoon on saucer. The room falls silent. The anticipation is palpable.

"Who is in third place" she asks audibly.

"In third place is....... " I pause for effect. "...... Nancy Jones".

Nancy Jones receives a potted house plant in an ornate holder amid a polite ripple of applause.

"Second place goes to ..... Doris Davies"

There is a minor rumpus when it is declared that Mrs Davies is a diabetic and the prize of a box of Bendicks Double Creams deemed wholly unsuitable for fear of a raise in her blood sugar, but calm is quickly restored when it is swapped for Mrs Jones' pot plant.

"And the winner is...... ". The room is silent for a moment. "........ Mrs Jessop".

Again the applause is polite more than thunderous but I think most people agreed that Mrs Jessop's creation of a bonnet in the shape of a topped off egg, with a spoon and two soldiers dressed as household guards standing up in it, was a witty and worthy winner.

"She was always good under the soldiers" quips Doreen Briggs.

"She could certainly make 'em stand to attention" continues Doreen Draper.

For myself, well..... I'll do anything for a walnut whip.

Klepto Chris

It is the day after a Bank Holiday.
I get a day in lieu because my normal day off each week is on Monday, so I save them all up throughout the year and take a week off, usually in November or if I am really fortunate in February.
The post is heavier than normal for a Tuesday after the extra day when only limited collections are gathered. It has been raining all night, the conditions are damp and grey, and the perky weathergirl on morning television says more precipitation is likely.
   I collect my special deliveries from Dave Tingly Tingle in the registered post counter, bundle up my bags, retrieve my wet weather coat from the locker, don my cycle helmet and set out aboard the trusty metal steed. The right pedal is slightly bent from when the wind caught the bike a low blow last week and blew it off its stand, and as the mechanism turns in an eccentric orbit it feels like I am riding with a limp .
   I free wheel down the slope away from the depot, brake to a halt at the junction with the main road and wait for an opportunity to join the traffic. I notice the standing water in the dip where the depot entrance meets the kerbside on the

High Street and see the number 47 coming towards me. Suddenly I am transfixed to the spot, unable to manouevre the bulk on the bike quickly enough and resign myself to the inevitable like a passenger in a car sliding on black-ice towards a wall. The bus swooshes past spraying the contents of the puddle in my general direction and I am helpless to evade it. Instinctively I turn my shoulder towards the assault and the deluge hits me with the force of the Angel Falls.

My expletive goes unheard by the driver as he presses on with his schedule and I am left standing beside my bike dripping heavily from the drenching. Perhaps I am imagining it but I am sure he had a grin on his face as he steered towards the standing water.

I shake myself down, shooing the water off my coat with the back of my hand as if I had eaten a particularily crumbly hobnob and decide to press on. The race is on to get done before the downpours commence, for every Postie will tell you that the job changes in the rain.

I race through the first bag of mail, refill from the side panniers and continue until I arrive outside number 104.

104 is a traditional three bed semi, built in the 1930s and unremarkable in its construction. The large bay window overlooks a neat front lawn with shrub laden borders on one side and a tarmac driveway down the other. The boundaries are marked by waist high wooden fences to keep out the neighbour's dog and children and the front brick wall adjacent to the pavement has chards of masonary falling off where the frost has gnawed at it over the years. The gatepost pillar provides a handy place to lean my bike so I park up.

A familiar face appears at the window anticipating my arrival.

I select my bundle from the mail bag peel off the red elastic bands and retrieve a small package from the rear pannier before striding up the drive towards the doorway. As I approach the open porchway the front door swings open and I am face to face with Christopher.

" Morning Christopher" I chirp.

" Morning Mickey. Have you got anything for me?"

Same greeting, same question every morning.

"Package for you Christopher, but you must sign for it"

"Oh right" says Christopher as if this is the first time we have been through the routine and I have caught him unprepared.

I pull out the pad and pen from my breast pocket and open the pad.

"Where do I sign?" Christopher asks remembering his lines.

"Right there" I say pointing at the second space on the sheet. "Number 2"

"Number 2?" repeats Christopher.

"Yer, right there" I say again placing my finger on the spot.

Christopher takes the pad and pen and leans on the window ledge for support.

"Number 2" he confirms to himself and begins to print his name slowly and deliberately.

I can see Mrs Price, Christopher's mother hovering by the kitchen door down the hallway keeping a watchful eye on events. I give her a quick wave and smile while Christopher completes his name.

"Do I have to sign now?" he asks continuing the double act.

"Just underneath your name" I respond.

"Just underneath my name" Christopher says to himself.

Christopher returns to his position by the window ledge and slowly signs his signature which bears a remarkable similarity to the printed version before he hands me back the pad and pen.

"Can I have my parcel now?" he almost pleads.

"Here you are" I say "And some letters for your mum"

He can hardly contain his excitement with the package and practically races down the hallway to offload the letters to his mum.

"What do you say to Mickey?" his mum gently chastises him.

"Thank you Mickey" he retaliates.

"You're welcome Christopher" I say.

Christopher was born prematurely and his brain was starved of oxygen.

It was touch and go as to whether or not he would survive and against low odds he pulled through.

He is twenty two now with the size and stature of a front row forward but with the mental capacity of the shirt number. He needs routines and structures, otherwise the frustrations he bears combined with the strength he possess can be an awesome combination, like an All-Black one score down with ten minutes to play.

Mrs Price is devoted to her son and pragmatic to his capabilities. Seemingly tireless in her support for Christopher it was with much relief when the post office decided not to prosecute and the package routine was contrived.

Christopher had become fixated with parcels and packages, stickers and stamps. One morning in the local post office he had taken a package which had been awaiting collection from off the counter.
The opportunity was fleeting like a mother stopping a pushchair beside the pick and mix in a supermarket and whilst she is deciding which sauce mix to have on the bolognese, her toddler is helping himself to gummy bears and fizzpops. The counter clerk had placed the parcel on the counter momentarily to clear space elsewhere and whilst Mrs Price was otherwise engaged with an adjacent clerk, temptation led Christopher to grasp the package and surreptitiously place it in his pocket.

After they left, the post office was in turmoil as the clerk began to doubt her sanity, a search of the premises was instigated and close circuit tapes monitored.

The first Mrs Price knew of the incident was when a patrol car pulled up outside the gate and uniformed officers knocked on the door. Her maternal instinct had told her that Christopher had been acting differently, and that she thought it slightly odd that he had wanted to play in his bedroom rather than help her make lunch as was the routine. Christopher had at first denied taking the the package as you would expect, but his chosen hiding place under his bed had not proved too challenging in retrieving the item.

Fortunately for Christopher, common sense prevailed and despite a severe ticking off from the Constables he was never charged, detained or convicted. The only damage done is that Mrs Price feels humiliated and embarrassed to ever set foot in the local post office again and now has to buy her stamps and postal orders in the next town. She is concerned however that Christopher may repeat his attempt at grand larceny and so the package routine was contrived.

    She moves down the hallway and gently says "It's working well".
    "Good" I reply "See you tomorrow"
    She hands me a carrier bag containing six small parcels all neatly wrapped in brown paper and cellotape. None have stamps stuck on or will go through a sorting office but each is addressed to C. Price.
    "For the next week" she says.

    Back at the depot we do our simple bit.
    Each parcel is embossed with meaningless rubber stamps before being placed in a redirection bag. As I leave each morning to start the walk, a blank signature card is obtained and completed except for item number 2.
    "........ And the special one for Klepto Chris" says Dave Tingly Tingle handing me the card each morning.

Albie

May. Tuesday. Sunny and bright.

The weather girl in a short skirt on Morning am says it will be "Scorchio".

I leave the depot in good time and wheel my way down to the start of my walk.

I am in shirt sleeves, and wear for Health and Safety reasons, a bright orange reflective jacket over my torso, which means I can be seen in Toronto. This jacket is particularily luminous having just been released from its cellophane wrapping, and makes the area under my chin look as if I have been Tangoed or too liberal with some fake tanning product. I may need shades tomorrow.

Some of my colleagues have decided summer is here and are giving their legs an airing. Donned in summer shorts and sporting albino knees they are sure to shock the neighbourhood. Ray 'Razor' Richards looks sensationally odd with his one chicken leg where the medical team shaved around the operating area before performing key-hole surgery on a troublesome cartilage, and the other so hairy it could easily pass for a grizzly's. There should be a law against *him* wearing shorts.

The schools are on half term holiday so the roads are quieter than normal as the volume of traffic takes a breather. The secondary school kids, usually loitering on the corner of Tiverton Grove waiting for the school bus, are notable by their absense and I do not have to run the daily gauntlet of blazered inertia as I avoid strewn school bags and Ipod wearing deaf-heads to reach the gate fronting Mrs Pendleton's garden. I post her copy of the Radio Times and move on.

Next door Tripod, Mrs Ogilvie's three legged, tortoise-shell cat, is hiding under the wheel of her Hyundai and I make some 'pss pss' noises as I try to encourage her towards me. Most times she purrs and rubs herself against my legs welcoming a quick stroke, but cats can be such indifferent creatures and today she just stares unblinking at me, reluctant to move except further into the shadows. There is only so long you can peer under a car without arousing suspicion so I press on.

I have been doing this walk for several years now and know the route like the back of my hand. Every now and then I stop to pick up stray red elastic bands which adorn the pavements and driveways and which take longer to disintegrate than a radioactive element's half life. Tazzzer covers my walk on a Monday, when I am off, and he feels obliged to leave me a trail to follow in case I get lost. He places the bands between his thumb and fore-finger and fires them off at random targets. Tripod quite often cops it, being as she is, one leg short of a quadruped and therefore a bit slower, and this might explain her reluctance to greet me in her usual fashion. I conclude it is either Tazzzer's sharp shooting or my eye popping, not yet sun-faded dayglo jacket.

    I move along Mulliner Road, and observe Mr Davies at number 45 as he is coming out of his front door.
"Don't be long" says a shrill voice. "Don't be long". Mr Davies stops on the threshold and leans back through the open doorway and counters with hint of exasperation, "Alright, alright, I won't be long."
    I approach him as he closes the door.
    "Worse than a wife" he shrugs.
    I smile and hand him his letters.
    I find it difficult to age certain people and Mr Davies falls into this category. He is long retired, five foot seven or eight inches tall, slightly stooped and pencil thin. He has a narrow face, sharp chin, and sprouts hair in small stubbly tufts from his ears and nostrils. He has mischievious, inquisitive eyes set under bushy eyebrows which dance around his forehead like two loved-up caterpillars about to commit the act. His laugh is infectious and eminates from somewhere deep within his frame, announcing itself in a gravelly gaffaw which makes me want to shake off my own inhibitions and join the party. He has deep wrinkly facial lines which move with every gesture and his mouth has age-yellowed teeth with noticeable gaps, like the ivories on an old piano. He wears the same patterned grey jumper and worn trousers from one day to the next, and compliments his generally unkempt appearance by a permanent three days growth.
    "Don't be long now" I say.
    "Don't you start" he retorts eyebrows already aroused.
    "Keeping tabs on you is he?"

"Might as well be tagged on my ankle"

Mr Davies is stepping out for his morning paper and a bottle of milk from the local newsagent. Inside Albie has to endure his own company for a few minutes until Mr Davies returns.

Albie is an African Grey, fifteen inches tall, with a light grey feathers on his body, darker grey ones on his wings and red tips to his tail. His wings have been clipped to stop him flying away but he still requires a large enviroment, daily stimulation and more entertaining than a two year old on Ribena. If Mr Davies neglects these responsibilities then Albie will become as bored as a teenager, get depression and start self-harming by plucking away his plummage. He is twenty one years old and has his birth certificated by the breeder. He can live upto 70 years which means he will probably see out Mr Davies and like many Greys he is extremely vocal with an extensive vocabulary and an ear for mimickery as good as any TV impressionist.

When he is hungry he calls " Albie likes nuts" or "Green grapes, green grapes"

He likes to show off and trills " Pssittacus Erithacus. Erithacus" using his latin name, and when he is wanting companionship he can swear like any Portugese sailor who reportedly brought back the first of the species from tropical West Africa. His cognative abilities are such that he can associate words or phrases with certain actions in the same way that dolphins, chimpanzees or nine year old humans can, and frequently makes sounds like a doorbell chiming, car alarm or Trevor McDonald on the News at Ten. Some of these birds have such a command of the language that they can hold a conversation, put together a coherent argument and complete The Times crossword in less than ten minutes.

    Albie watches from his cage in prime position by the window as Mr Davies and I chat.
    He is incapable of being domesticated so always has the upper hand. He watches us as if he knows it. Should his keeper be too long at the newsagent Albie will have torn the place apart with a beak as sharp as any tin opener and deficated anywhere and everywhere.
    He taps his beak on the window as if to say "For pity's sake. It's *just* the post"
    "Better go" says Mr Davies. "See you tomorrow"
    "Don't be long" I repeat mimicking an African Grey.

Ronnie....The Rocket

Wednesday. The rain is a deluge, like someone has turned on the sprinkler system over the UK to drench, and then gone out for the day.

The perky weather girl on morning am suggests a brolly, but then she does not have to hump around six to eight heavy sacks of post, and ride a bike.

I trudge into the depot after my short ride from home, already wetter than I would care to be.

"Still raining out there?" asks Tazzzer as I peel off my protective gear leaving a trail of drips across the floor. " I *hate* it when it rains" he adds and dumps a bundle of post onto his work station with undue force emphasising his frustration with the climate.

"In for the day according to the forecast" I say.

"All day?"

" Yep. Think so. Certainly when we're out and about"

"I *bloody* hate this job in the rain" spouts Tazzzer and I fear for his next bundle of mail.

In truth he is only uttering what every Postie will tell you. The job changes dramatically when you are trying desperately to keep dry Mr Jones' hospital appointment letter, or preventing Mrs Smith's water bill from looking like she has just received a free sample. On fine days

Posties cannot wait to vacate the depot and press on with their walks, but on a day like this there is always time for another cup of tea in the hope that a constant downpour turns to steady rain, or steady rain turns to light drizzle, or drizzle turns to occasional showers before time presses on and we have no option but to leave.

Dazzer sidles up to me.

"Have you got something for The Rocket? He retires on Saturday."

A discreet manilla envelope is held gaping in front of me and I reach inside my trouser pocket and pull out a note.

"What are you going to get him?" I ask.

"I spoke to his missus and she said to get him an ipod. That way he can play his own music and she doesn't have to listen to it as well. There's a card doing the rounds somewhere. Give it back to me once you've signed it will you."

Dazzer trundles off to find his next donor. Most will contribute.

The Rocket is an old stager and popular with most of his colleagues. Whenever there is a piece of post with an indecipherable address, or a street name with no number, the rest of us Posties can rely on The Rocket to say where it should be delivered. Having worked so long for the Post Office he is like a back catalogue of place names, customers details, house addresses, route maps, drop off points, collection times, all the little details that make the depot flow. You could literally send an envelope addressed only to Fred and The Rocket would give you a list of addresses where Fred might reside before topping it off with:

"It's probably Fred So and so at such and such address. It was his birthday on Monday. Going by the post mark I bet that is from his brother in Reading"

He has worked man and boy on the mail, first on an apprentice round, then covering a multitude of walks, before inheriting walk 23 and making it his own. For the past two decades or more he has delivered the post to the same set of addresses most mornings and has become a familiar sight to the customers he serves. Some will miss him for his friendliness, others for his punctuality, and still others for his neighbourliness. Many a time he has helped someone out, like when Mrs Patterson locked herself out and he showed remarkable capabilities as a cat burglar and helped her gain an entry, or when Mr McMillan fell over on the ice and The Rocket picked him up and made sure he and his shopping got home safely. Some people will miss him just for his regularity, like a well worn routine that you take comfort from and rely upon. Same place, same time.

Saturday comes around. Weather dry. Sky overcast.

"30 per cent chance of precipitation" says the smarmy young weather man hedging his bets on morning am. The Rocket's last day.

I cycle to the depot as usual, sign on and gather by the sorting area ready for his presentation.

All the crew are gathered, one or two have even come in on their day off just to see The Rocket take off. Len has to go through some other matters first.

"Er....Firstly....er....Region are stamping down on cycle

helmets again." He starts shuffling his papers. He always has an air of uncertainty when holding meetings like this, and his body language betrays his discomfort while speaking in public.

"Makes a change from them kicking us in the nuts" pipes a voice from the back amid sniggers of approval.

"They are... er...going to remove the bikes from anyone caught riding without their crash top....er ..this has already happened in one location " continues Len ignoring his heckler, "...... So don't be a prat and wear your hat." The line goes down well as a ripple of laughter goes around the meeting and Len warms to his audience.

"Dickie's already one" chirps Phil Philly Metcalfe who has an ongoing feud with Dickie Pratt.

"I'm also a Dick" counters Dickie.

"So does that mean that we have to keep putting on and taking off our helmets as we go round" accuses Mad Mick Maloney.

"No it just means you have to put it on...." says Len "....When you ride your bike".

"Yer and what if we are walking up driveways ...."

Most meetings start well and descend rapidly into a barrage of "what if " questions and sometimes Len's patience is tested to the limit. We know he is exasperated when he resorts to the line "Just use your own common sense" a commodity in very short supply with some of my colleagues.

Presently, the business end of the meeting done, Len turns his attentions to The Rocket. He salutes his service with a few chosen words and the cliched clock for the mantle-piece, before handing him the card and gift from his colleagues.

The Rocket takes it all in his stride.

His leaving speech is structured and brief Understandably he reminisces about the old post office and the good old days before concluding.

"..........over the years I have delivered tens of thousands of letters and packets to thousands of people. Even today I find myself with a walk with a multitude of trades. I have a Carpenter, two Millers, a Woodman and a Silversmith. Of people with rank there is a King, a scottish monarch.....a Mc..Queen," There is an audible groan, ".... a Regent and an ex president.....Gerald Ford. The clergy is represented with two Bishops, a Rector, a couple of Priests and a family of Popes. I deliver to all the colours of the spectrum....Green, Black, White, Brown and Grays. Ornithologically there are Sparrows, Eagles and Crows.....but only the other day I have taken on a new resident with inter-galactic tendancies.....a ..Dr Hew. It has been a pleasure to serve them all."

As the applause die away and individuals peel away after wishing The Rocket a well earned retirement one thing is sure.

The Rocket will miss delivering the mail more than the Royal Mail will miss him. One retired full timer replaced by one and a half part-timers on reduced hours. Redistribututunion of his old walk is the future. Larger walks with fewer people. Rationalisation. Privatisation? Redistribution of key resources. New technology replacing old, tried and trusted ways.

Some of his customers will not now get their post until mid afternoon ..... but that is progress.

Other books by Mickey Mack

It's Just The Post   vol 1

It's Just The Post   vol 2

It's Just The Post   vol 3

It's Just The Post   vol 4

It's Just The Post   Children's Edition

It's In The Post

All available at:

www.amazon.co.uk
www.lulu.com
www.itsjustthepost.co.uk

www.ingramcontent.com/pod-product-compliance
Lightning Source LLC
Chambersburg PA
CBHW061247040426
42444CB00010B/2279